What I Would Leave for My Family

Prince Morara Moshoeshoe
moraram@princemorara.com

Visit www.booksurge.com to order additional copies.

What I Would Leave for My Family

What I leave for my family
BEFORE I SHIP OUT

Prince Morara

2007

What I Would Leave for My Family

BOCHABELA

A long time ago, my grandfather founded my country Bocha-bela. This was a very difficult time. Wars were occurring everywhere. People were fighting for food and to keep their land. There were two major powers, the Zulus and Chaka against the Boers. On one side, nations were fleeing from Chaka's spear, and on the other side they were being persecuted by the Boers, who were trying to take over their land.

Eventually, they succeeded in conquering all of the black nations, including the Zulus. However, there was one small nation called the Babohlale nation, which was ruled by my great-grandfather, King Morara. He fought the Boers and many others, including King Monaha. The defeat was so spectacular that his people said he shaved his beard. King Morara was loved by his people, especially the poor. They called him *Morara o leseli o bone la marena o mafutsana a shoeleng a u luma*, which means "sweet grapes which the poor died praising."

Since he was the only one left, the Boers mounted a fierce campaign against him and cornered him on top of a small, but flat mountain. It was on this mountain that King Morara fought bravely, and the Boers were unable to extricate him. They decided to wait him out. After several weeks, he started to run out of supplies and water for the livestock, so he turned to his white missionary friends for help. They advised him to declare himself part of Bahlapi (a large European country). King Morara took their suggestion and declared himself Mohlapi. The leader of the Bahlapi (fish eaters), then sent a message to the Boers to leave King Morara alone.

The Boers retreated, allowing King Morara and his people some room. Later, the leader of Bahlapi sent a representative to draw new borders. This representative gave away most of our land. The people were so angry with him, that they called him *Majoro oa tena* or "major who made us fed up." The river that became the border is called Moo-Ka-hare, which means "here inside!"

King Morara was grateful to the Bahlapi for getting rid of the Boers. As a sign of his gratitude, he sent his son Masia (my grandfather) to study medicine overseas. While he was studying, a war broke out in Europe. There was also a cruel leader of Manasi who tried to take over Bahlapi country. My grandfather was asked to quit school and come home to lead the African soldiers, because most of them did not want to go to war against Manasi.

My grandfather Masia led his people to battle and fought bravely. However, the Manasi captured him and some of his men, because they had pushed too far into the enemy territory. He was able to successfully negotiate a surrender to protect his men from being killed by the Manasi soldiers. My grandfather was always eager to learn, and he quickly learned how to speak Nasi. He was then recruited to work for them by selling fruits in the streets to raise money for their war.

After several years, the Manasi lost the war, and my grandfather and his men were released. During his time there, he had a Nasi wife, which he kept secret. After his release from prison, he was unable to pick up his Nasi wife. He was only able to sneak out a good buy. When he arrived at her place, she was very happy to see him. However, he told her that the war was over, and that he was free, but the Bahlapi had asked everybody to sail back home to Africa. And since he was a leader and future king, he had to go. He promised her that he would write and find a way for her to come to Africa.

This sounded like a good plan, except that she was not buying it. She cried and cried.. After awhile, with his man calling him and saying, "Let's go, let's go, or we are going to run into some Manasi, or miss our boat home," she revealed some shocking news. In an effort to make him stay, she told him, "I am having a baby." My grandfather replied, "I cannot make a baby now, I have to go. They are waiting for me." She rubbed her eyes, pulled her hair into a ponytail, and said, "I am pregnant." My grandfather jumped with shock and excitement and said, "Did you say you are pregnant?"

This child would be my grandfather's firstborn and, as such, a future king. My grandfather was distressed and they both cried. It was difficult for him to explain to his father about the child. It was even harder for his Nasi wife, because she had no husband and was carrying a black child. My grandfather ran to a Bahlapi captain and asked him for advice. He told him to send her to America, where there should be less problems for them. The couple took a collection and had enough money for her boat ride to the States.

My grandfather and his men sailed back to Africa. He tried to go back to Bahlapi to finish medicine, but there was no money and his father was getting too old. My grandfather, with the help of the Bahlapi, established the first Bochabela police force and formed the Bochabela Defense Force. When his father died, he was passed over, and the throne was given to his younger brother. He was said to be more qualified because he stayed by his father's side and learned how to govern, whereas my grandfather was said to be too European and warlike. My grandfather remarried and held a few government posts, but his mind remained in the military where he retired.

After my father finished high school, my grandfather sent him to Bahlapi to study medicine. He agreed, but after the first year in college he dropped out, married a Hlapi girl, and joined the Scotland Yard police force. He was there for seven years and became a fingerprint expert. After Botswana gained its independence, he was recalled home. His father was upset with him, but he left and went to train Botswana's first police force. There is a woman detective there who has our name, and she tells a story in a book about her father or our father.

After establishing the Botswana police force, he joined the South African police. This was during the apartheid. He acted as a liaison between the white police force and the black people. He communicated with the blacks what the whites were grumbling about. And he explained or taught the whites how to work with black leaders. He was such a success that when a paramount chief Kaiser Matanzima was in danger due to a family feud, the white government sent him to Transkei to protect him and to train their police force.

While working in South Africa as a police officer, he married his best friend's sister. This act was also in retaliation because his best friend (now my uncle), married his former girlfriend. When he found out, he went and asked one of his best friend's sisters to marry him. Surprisingly, she said yes even though they never dated. He took his new bride to South Africa. The couple had John, my oldest brother; Samuel, my elder brother; and me. I was given the name Liteboho, which as a prayer to say, "Enough boys, God, now we are praying for girls." Then my younger sister was born. She is Lisebo, which means "people are gossiping."

While in the police force, my father studied the Bible, and after being ordained, he joined the South African Defense Force and was the first black army chaplain. Later, the white South African government sent him back to Transkei to train their soldiers. His friend Kiser Matanzema became the leader of Transkei, and my father had fun training soldiers during the day and teaching the Bible to Xhosas in the villages. At this time, I was now in college in Bochabela. However, before then I remember living in Bloemfontein. Then I was sent to Tsikoane in Bochabela. This is where finished first grade.

I stayed with my grandfather from my mother's side. They all loved me, and I had so much fun. I was a brave little man. I remember climbing all the way to the top of the mountain at night by myself. I went to gather our cattle, but I was too young to tell time. So I just went, and by the time I reached the foot of the mountain, it was dark. However, my eyes had adjusted to the darkness, so I just kept on climbing. When I came back home, everybody was looking for me and had no idea where I went. I was not sure, but I think after that situation, I was sent to live with my grandmother from my father's side. Also, I think I was sent away because my aunt got married, and it was getting harder for my grandfather Ntate Gilbert Motolo to take care of me.

Being sent to Mathokoane to live with my brothers whom I did not know and my grandmother that I had never seen before did not make me a happy camper. I am still a little ticked off about it. When my grandfather took me there, we rode on his beautiful horse. Then he told me I had to stay there, because they needed me to help look after their cattle. He promised he was going to come and get me before the school opened.

Indeed, one day I looked up and saw his horse. I just took off and left the cattle in the fields with Samuel. I was so happy that I was finally going home. When I reached him, I hugged him (it makes me tear up just think about it). I did not want to sit or wait for him to finish talking. I was ready to go. I had a bunch of stories to take home with me. I was so homesick. I did not want to have anything to do with this place. I am sure Ntate Gilbert was in tears when he had to explain to me that he just brought my clothes and that I would be staying and going to school there.

He loved me so much he called me Lapotlaka Lehlanya, meaning a "fast grassy man." He took me wherever he went. We looked after his cattle together. I remember always laughing because he was always making jokes. I miss him very much. He and my grandmother passed away one after the other. I remember because my grandmother from my father's side was talking about how they called each other. I do not remember who passed away first.

A few years ago, I was given the best honor ever, which was to participate in building their house. I was so grateful that the Lord gave me this opportunity. I was so grateful that the Lord has favored me. From when I was very little, I could pray a personal prayer. My grandmother used to call us to pray every evening. She told us about stories in the Bible, even though I do not remember her reading one. The story that I have never forgotten is of Joseph and his brothers, how his father loved him so much that it made his brothers jealous. I remember many times praying that I could be like him.

As much as I loved Tsikoane, I quickly made new friends when the school opened. The teachers just loved me, especially the principal. She begged my father to let me stay with her. I must have been very small because she called me Leqa or Tsuonyana (little meat or chicken), so quiet and innocent. We walked at least ten miles one way to school, but we had fun.

5

Here, unlike in Tsikoane, there were not any girls living with us. In order to compensate for the lack of girls, my grandmother taught us how to clean and cook. We used to alternate between taking the cattle out to the pastures and staying at home to fetch water form the river, cleaning, making beds and cooking. My grandmother was a very good teacher, because she was very patient with us, especially to me. She used to look at me and start laughing, and say, "Ngoana ngoanaka (grandchild), "you look just like your parents." She told me this every day. Oh! She never spanked me, or I don't remember. I was always very attentive to details. My grandmother showed me how to do something only once, and I would eagerly try to do it just the way she showed me. However, in most cases it would not be perfect because it would either be too heavy or too hot for me to carry or handle.

My uncle Michael also preferred to go and work in the fields with me, even though I was too little to handle the oxen, which we used for plowing. If he took any of my big brothers, he would come home upset, saying they don't listen. Michael had to keep telling them the same thing over and over again.

In Tsikoane, we had Abuti Thabo to look after the cattle while we went to school, but here I went to school every other day, alternating with my elder brother. We must have been in the same class because we took notes for each other. However, one year he went to the next class and I was told to repeat my grade. I was not happy, but they convinced me that it would be fun because I already know the material. So I said, "Cool, I don't have to work hard next year. I am going to have fun." I am glad they did that because after that, I was an A student and never looked back.

One year my father dropped by and took us to another school. I believe I was in the fifth grade and Sam was in the sixth. This was a Catholic school, and my father had to fight to get us in. But once we were in Ntate Makatse, the principal loved us. He said we were very disciplined. Again, the Lord showed me His mercy when I met a Boy Scout master nicknamed Tshola uJe, which means, "Set the table and eat." He was skinny, but fast and strong. I don't know why they associated him with food. He was such a smart guy; more importantly, he was very kind. I was like a little puppy to him—everywhere he went I followed. He really loved me. He taught me honor, trust, duty, and kindness, because of his teaching I was very well liked and trusted by everybody including Bishop Khoarai. I used to take walks with him.

When I got to Sacred Heart High School, I was still an A student. As a freshman I became one of the editors of the school paper. After the second year, the principal, Brother Henry, hired me as his assistant. I prepared the report cards and assisted him with the office work. When he would go on vacation, he used to leave me in charge of the school. He only gave me two instructions, "Double lock the office, and please do not admit any new students." He put so much trust in me. Since then, there is no job I am afraid to do. The Lord is always with me. He is always with me. I was loved and trusted. That's an awesome blessing there.

I also had the best teachers, namely Brother Martel; Mr. Rampeta, who is now the principal; Brother Herry, the former principal; Ms. Coney, Mrs. Moholisa and Musuoe Lesitsi, who in my opinion is the best teacher ever. Somehow, I did end up staying by myself. Samuel and my mother left and found my father in Transkei. So Mosuoe Lesitsi had to take care of me, like I was his own only son. He is my neighbor, so he had to teach me at school and at home. I had no idea what I was doing, but I know that he loved me, and in return I made sure that I received A's on his tests and exams. Mosue Lesitsi is a great man, a wonderful teacher and the greatest parent. How can I ever repay the amount of time he spent on me? With him, I am truly blessed.

After high school, my father told me to close my store or shop and go to the university to study medicine. He said when I was young, I got very sick. He took me to a doctor who was drunk and gave me the wrong medication. I was so sick that they had to take me to the ER (emergency room) where they pumped my stomach. Then my father said he made a promise to God that if I make it, he will make sure I became a doctor. I closed my store and went to do medicine, even though I was very good in business and accounting.

Since there were no medical schools in Bochabela, I had to apply to Watts, which is in South Africa. Whenever the school received my application and grades, they would say, "Well done, but you have to get police clearance first before we can issue your admission." When I went to the police, they would say, "No, get admitted first, then we will look into your clearance." This went on until I finished pharmacy. Then I reapplied hoping this time they are going to admit me, but instead, they gave me the same story.

Then I got a job as a pharmacist in Butha-Buthe. I was there for a few months, when the local politicians came knocking at my door. My uncle Jonathan, who was then the prime minister, felt that I did not show enough support for him. My father had instructed me to keep my head in the sciences and to never touch politics, so I did not go to any party meetings or demonstrations. Then one day, one of my coworkers came and told me that I should pack my things and leave, because they were planning to kill me. She begged me to leave. She even offered me money for transportation. She said, "If you don't want to leave, remove your important documents like passports and certificates, because they are coming to destroy you."

Being a brave fool, I said, "Yea, yea, thanks, but no thanks." Ten o'clock sharp as I laid in the dark fully dressed with my eyes wide open and wishing for a quick-dawn arrival, I heard about twenty boots matching toward my room. They went *Boom, boom!* I sat up with my eyes piercing in the dark like a mouse. With lights off, I thought that they would think I was not home. When they kicked the door, I jumped, but somehow I did not make any noise. However, cold sweat ran down my spine. Thanks to whoever installed the door because it did not fly open.

My hunters had a bunch of keys which they tried one by one. The last key went in, but it did not unlock the door. Then they shuffled them and tried another one. It went in, *koatla koatla!* However, the door did not swing open. This went on as I sat at the edge of my single bed shivering and trembling. *Shwahla shwahla!* The keys jangled as they selected another one. Names, different names they were angrily calling me, literally trying to dig me out like a fox digging for a mouse. It knows the mouse is in there. It can smell it, and it keeps digging.

Shwehle-shwehle, Nyene nyene! The sound of my key dislodged to the floor. I jumped, and swiftly I was on my knees, sweeping the floor briskly with my hand. *Ting!* I found it. Quickly but silently, I stuck it back and held it in place. I stood there with my eyes tightly shut. Somehow, this silenced my huffing and puffing. Key to key, the battle went on for eternity. Stronger name-calling, then I heard a soft voice begging, "Let's go, we will catch him later." It repeated, "We will definitely catch him later. Just like a hurricane, they stormed away, and I went, *Hugh, Hugh!* Like a hare or rabbit after being chased by a coyote. I put my ear to the crack in the door, and for about a minute I heard nothing.

I don't remember where my passport and certificates were, but when I left they were with me. I was so scared that I could see in the dark. I said my prayer and turned the key, nothing blew up, or slammed the door, so I cracked the door open, and took off hopping from shadow to shadow, as I scanned the yard. Nothing but silence. In the nearby pine trees I melted in the darkness. One hour later, I came to rest at a high school. As I was cutting through the dark, with my chest out and my ears pinned back, I believe I heard somebody closing in on me.

I found an unlocked classroom and checked in for the night. Very early when it was still dark, I went back to the hospital to leave the keys to the pharmacy and a note to the staff that it was nice knowing them. I was on the first bus out of town and left the country. I caught another bus from Ficksburg to Bloemfontein, where I met with my father. Then I got on another bus to Umtata, Transkei. I don't remember if somebody met me at the bus station, but somehow I made it to our house. My mother was in Leribe, Bochabela, and my dad I had just left in Bloemfontein, where he was attending some conference. My elder brother Samuel was there, because I remember him proudly introducing me saying, "Le ndota eza komfa kwam (this man comes after me)."

The house was nice, huge and clean. The streets were well lit. This was a white neighborhood. I enjoyed that place. I met new people and made a lot of friends. I felt like a movie star. After a few weeks, my father found me a job at Umtata General Hospital Pharmacy. I ran the surgical store with my best friend Chief Mgolobane. The work was fun, but the money was lousy. When the university reopened, I enrolled in science. Again, I applied to Watts, thinking now they will take me because I am in a South African college. It did not work! They gave me the same story, so I just kept busy with biology, chemistry, some physics and math. I was hoping that one day something will change.

HOW I GOT HERE.

There was a strike at University of Transkei. Students refused to attend classes. I think they were striking about the cafeteria food. However, they ate the food every day but did not attend classes. Few days later, my father gave us a warning to stay at home because the police were coming. Yes, they did show up one early morning. They whipped the students through the campus. When the dust settled, they sent everybody home and closed the university for two weeks.

My brother, Mongaka had an idea that we should go to America while the school is closed. We pushed and pressed until we received a visa and came to the States. This was one very long journey. We arrived in New York at about 2 p.m. From the plane, New York looked like a bunch of small islands. My expectation was that the USA would be a very clean place with tall glass buildings and no dust on the streets just like the inside of a shopping mall. Somehow, we proceeded all the way out to the taxi rank. This tall black guy approached us and said, "Need a cab?" I looked at the streets and buildings, and there was dust everywhere. Some of the buildings were old and made out of red bricks. I asked the guy, "Is this Washington DC?" He said with a deep but polite voice, "This is New York, you need to go back inside and catch another plane to DC." So we pushed our way back in. The customs officer asked, "Where are you going? You cannot come back this way." I said, "We are going to Washington DC." So he sent us to a ticket counter to buy tickets to DC.

After a couple of hours, we were off to DC. When we arrived in Washington, I was relieved to find that the place was very clean. I said to myself, "This is what I expected." While in DC we stayed with Ntate Tim. He was shocked when we called him from National airport. He told us to take a cab to Gallows road, in Fairfax County, where he lived. We stayed with him for a few weeks and looked for schools. Strayer College was the first one to admit us. Then we hopped on a TrailWays bus and visited Virginia Commonwealth University (VCU) in Richmond, Virginia. When we arrived downtown the sun was already going down. We walked up Broad Street. On both sides people were lined up for city buses to take them home. I said to my brother, "We came to the wrong city." He said, "Why?" I said, "I think this a black town. It is so different from DC. Look how many Blacks they have lined up on both sides of the street for blocks."

In the morning, we started at Virginia Union thinking it would be easier to get in, but they did not want to have anything to do with us. So we went to Virginia Commonwealth University (VCU). The admission officer was a black lady named, Laura. We did not know what to think after coming from the apartheid system. I was conditioned to see everything in black versus white. But Ms. Laura gave me my first taste of freedom. She was very professional and gracious. She asked us to take a placement test. After which she admitted us. I could not believe it. I called my father and was hysterical. A White school had admitted us, without questions about police clearances. I said to myself, "I love this country." This was the America that I was dreaming about, a place where people act and treat you professionally. I finally felt that I was somebody. I called my father with the good news and asked for more money.

Brother Mpheteng, who had come down to VCU with us, introduced us to Mr. and Mrs. Meade, a wonderful couple. They helped us get situated in the school dormitory and with class registrations. From day one, Mr. and Mrs. Meade treated us like their sons. From the minute we met them, they became our American family. They provided us guidance, food, clothing, money, and most of all, they gave us unconditional love. They sincerely cared about us. There was nothing we could offer them but a simple thank you and a sense of great appreciation. They made us comfortable and confident. I faced schoolwork and whatever else I went through, knowing that they had my back. I listened to their advice and was always willing to learn from them. I had no reason to think or feel they had an ulterior motive.

WHAT I WOULD LEAVE FOR MY FAMILY

When Mr. Meade passed away, I bought his car. And when Mrs. Meade moved to a nursing home, she sold me her house. There were many things that she did for me which, like any child, you do not see everything your parents do for you, and this includes praying for you. When an elderly person kneels down and says a prayer for you, this is bigger than winning the lotto or getting a doctorate degree. You get blessed beyond your imagination. Their prayers continue to produce blessings for the rest of your life. I wish I had done more for them. In my heart, I have no doubt that I loved them as their son. Indeed, I have found favor in the Lord. His mercy followed me from Africa to America. Every day the Lord continues to show me His love and mercy. I hope one day I get a chance to share it with somebody. I hope one day I become a blessing to somebody.

Unlike in the movie *Coming to America*, I did find my bride in Ashland, Virginia, not in Queens. I do not remember Mr. and Mrs. Meade's reaction, except they loved my children and wife. I am not sure how my father felt when he found out. However, I am sure my mother had to do a lot of explaining and reassuring, that I was going to be okay with my American bride. Well, as in *Coming to America*, now my father loves my wife and his grandchildren just as if the whole thing were planned by him. I know my actions did cause him a lot of headaches. I just hope I can do something nice to make him forget all those worries. It will be like seeing your infant baby smile; you forget all their crying and temper tantrums and just enjoy their simple smile.

Now I have children of my own, and last Sunday, I took my oldest daughter, Senate to Chowan University in North Carolina. Like a good parent, I suggested that she attend a college here in Richmond, Virginia, but that did not quite work. When I had to pay all that money, I remember the changes I put my father through by coming here. However, nothing was going to stop me from taking my baby to college, to see her in her dormitory room and to give her a hug, take pictures and give here my last hundred, including my credit card. I am very proud of her. She looked so happy. I am glad that she did not see me cry. I love her very much. May the Lord bless her and keep her safe.

I do thank the Lord for making it possible. Before leaving, the family got together, and we thanked God. I prayed in Sesotho, because this time I wanted the Lord to know that I was sincerely grateful. The prayer was deep from my heart. I did not want to mispronounce some English words and lose my thoughts. Indeed, the Lord continues to show me His love and mercy.

A few weeks before Senate was born, I shipped out to Great Lakes for boot camp. I wanted to make sure I had a solid job, so that my family will be well taken care of. I did not know what to expect except that I had a good reason and was more than prepared mentally. I also planned to have fun, as I saw how my father enjoyed his military career. Other than when my children were born, my best day in this country was when I was in a U.S. uniform. In boot camp, everybody received the same training. Every color, height, weight, attitude got the same treatment. As sailors, we were molded into one color, navy blue.

When we looked at each, we only saw someone that we could depend on. We totally believed in each other, the Navy, and this great country, the USA. Even in my sleep I dream of defending this country. Now, the USA, is where I live, this is where my children and my wife live. I have news for those who wish to harm us. Don't even think about it. Stay away from the schools where my children go. Stay away from their school buses. Stay away from my metro or subway, which I take to work. Definitely stay away from our malls where my wife does her therapy shopping.

America and England measure their responses to would-be terrorists, but I will not. So you better take notice that when England fights, I fight. When you mess with America, you are messing with my family, and that's personal. I pray for the salvation of would-be bad guys' and God's mercy. It is better to seek the Lord than to make war with one's neighbors. When we find God, we find love.

After completing the navy training, I requested orders to a very far place from the USA, but instead, I was sent to National Naval Medical Center, in Bethesda. Here the Lord blessed me with promotions and responsibilities. I was responsible for supplying the outlining clinics with pharmaceuticals. Most importantly, I was responsible for compounding. I made creams, lotions, ointments, and oral suspensions. I also did a tour at the Pentagon. This was a dream job, and I felt so blessed. Here I had some of the best leaders. A Jewish colonel, Dr. Block, was smart, nice, and had a great sense of humor. My supervisor was a Filipino lady. She was tough, but very fair. If she were not a civilian, she would have been a general.

I was blessed in Africa, but I have been blessed even more here in America. A challenge or discomfort sometimes, it gives one an opportunity for change or improvement. If you look for the most advanced person of color, you will find him in the States, yet their history is the most painful. After more than twenty years, Mandela came out of jail and became one of the most respected world leaders.

A very senior White House official needed a bone marrow transplant. After testing about a quarter million white servicemen, there was no match. Then the commander was encouraged to test anybody who volunteered. Most people of color kept away. However, two weeks later, a word came down that a match had been found. Everybody was delighted. Sadly, a rumor started circling that further tests were needed because the match was highly unlikely or improbable. This was sad and confusing.

It was in the afternoon when my commander called me to his office. When the commander singles you out and calls you to his office, it is usually not a good thing. You come to work and do your very best, and the rest will take care of itself. From the compounding room to his office, I went through every possible thing that I had done. I went through all of the scenarios that my mind could process. When I entered the office, my chief was there, which usually means you are in trouble when you are called to the old man's office and your chief is already there! The assistant commander was also there. Then there were two high-ranking officers, which I had never met.

I was scared and shaking. My eyes were rapidly filling with tears. Before the commander said, "Have a seat; it is okay, do not be scared," tears were already running down my cheeks. I cried because I did not want to disappoint my commander, or my family. All I ever wanted to hear after work is "Job well done." Then I am out of there. I was still too confused, but I heard the captain say something about classified information and some tests that I have to take and that I am to tell no one. I just agreed and said, "Aye-aye, sir."

I was escorted to some doctor's consulting room where I signed a bunch of papers without question. I was just relieved that I had not done anything wrong. The doctor took a bunch of samples. After that, I was admitted or kept at the hospital. Later I looked at my chief and signaled that I did not know what was going on. He just said, "Don't worry about it, you will be okay. " For two days I stayed there in isolation. I had some officer who kept me company. But at the door they posted a guard at all times. The officer checked everything they brought to my room. If a nurse wanted to check my vital signs, he made sure to check the equipment.

On the third day in the morning, my commander, a doctor, two very senior officers, and my chief came to my room. I was scared, but eager to hear the next step, whether they will say, "You are free to go home," or "we need more tests," or "we are transferring you to another facility." After they all settled down, the commander announced that I was a perfect match. He said they didn't know why but those were conclusive results. I was so relieved because finally I had an idea of what was going on. I was happy and agreed to do whatever they were asking me. I signed more papers, but none said I could leave. I was told the White House was very glad that I agreed to help him.

I donated the bone marrow, and the high official's illness went away. About four months later, I was invited to the White House. Now that was so cool! I enjoyed the visit. When I got home, the media was waiting for me with cameras, lights, microphones, and a bunch of questions, all asked at the same time. I kept saying, "No comment please, no comment." One persistent reporter kept saying, "Are you related, are you related?" I told her no comment, but I thought maybe we are related. You know, my grandfather's first child from his German wife was born here. "Hum!" Well, I am just happy I could help. I will leave the investigation or digging to the reporters.

I have since left the service and the White House official was instrumental in helping me start my Metr-O-ffice Shuttle business. The business was so successful that I was able to turn it into a franchise. I have also been able to start other businesses. I am very glad that I was a match. I am very glad I could help my American cousin. He has since visited my country and has established an HIV AIDS foundation. I really appreciate his help. He is a great blessing to my people. May the Lord continue to bless him and his family.

In his home state, where he grew up, they don't like him very much. In fact, a good number of Americans will throw eggs at him and chase him away. It is not that he did anything wrong; they just hate him. So beware that in your hometown a lot of people may call you crazy, and plot to lock you up, or put you in a nut house. They may criticize everything you say. However, in another town they may see you as a hero. As much as America does not like him, the rest of the world welcomes him with open arms. He is regarded as one of our best modern leaders.

TO SENATE (TSOMPI-TSOMPI)

I leave you the beach house (six bedrooms), and the condominium. Please take good care of the workers, and they will take care of you. I have arranged for their retirement.

I am leaving you my BMW and the Hummer II. Remember to wear a seatbelt, and to look carefully when changing lanes. Let somebody else pump gas for you. Do not play your stereo too loud.

You could stay at the condo until you get married, and then move to the beach house. Marry somebody serving in the Naval Reserve Medical Core. If they do not want to serve the country, would they fight for you? I have arranged for your honeymoon in South Africa. The air there is much fresher, especially in the morning. You may have only three children.

Visit Africa once a year. Take Thabiso with you. He will look out for you. Do not dismiss the drivers. Take Joseph because he is a very good driver. Pay him well and travel with him. I also leave you the second store. Keep the manager. He is an honest man. Let him run the store.

Support the Scott's Hospital, in Lesotho. Build a new wing for children, and make sure it is well equipped. I would like you also to give support to the Mathokoane Primary School. Remember to work along with the embassy and support people from home.

I leave you my bodyguard. Do not fire him. He made a commitment to me. Do not go anywhere without a bodyguard. You must have two very good friends. Always wear a full dress, preferably black, blue, or any reddish solid color. Watch out for high heels. Always wear comfortable shoes. You might need to stand up for yourself or walk away from a bad situation.

Do not miss breakfast. No breakfast or a bad one may spoil your day. Always have your assistant introduce you. Speak only when you have everybody's attention. Do not let anyone interrupt you. Choose your words wisely. No small talk and no jokes. Be comfortable with what you say. Do not make a comment unless you are sure about the facts. Speak only in statements. Never say you don't know. Just say, "My assistant is preparing a reply, and I will be happy to answer you as soon as we are ready." Remember, you must check your facts. Do not say it, if you are not sure.

I leave you the family credit union or bank. You will find the manager very helpful. Attend all board meetings. Find out what the growth rate is. I set it up for a 7 percent growth rate. Make smart loans. If you cannot repossess it, do not finance it. Also, if it does not gain value, do not finance. You may review the loans, but do not process them. Remember, you own the bank, you do not work there.

Avoid media or publicity. They are always looking for something negative. Attend only formal gatherings. Always be punctual, but leave as early as possible. Do not go to bed tired. Always have a bath and eight hours of sleep. Too much work for you means your assistant messed up the schedule.

Always leave at least one hour for prayer. First, thank God that you are able to pray or talk to him. Then thank Him, because you are alive and beautiful. Thank Him for clean water, good food, new shoes and everything you have. Ask Him to bless you with wisdom, good health, a beautiful smile, and a nice figure (even though you always complain that you do not have enough secrets to put inside the Victoria Secret).

Ask Him to bless your brothers and sisters. Ask Him to bless the police, firefighters and their families. Ask Him to bless hospital works. Ask Him to bless our leaders. Pray that our leaders prepare us for the hereafter, or the coming of the Lord. I wonder if Jesus would need clearance to land at the Reagan National Airport. Ask Him to always be with you and walk with you. Ask Him to always make you an asset to His kingdom. Thank Him for being able to wake up. Always be ready to do His will.

Do the sign of cross as often as you can. It's a way to wave at Him or to say, "Hello, I am here, please be with me." Let Him speak through you, so you may not waste time with fruitless speeches. Do this in a quiet place, and let no one disturb you when praying.

No flirting with men. They should bow and kiss your hand. You are the future queen, so start acting like one. Do not go to a meeting unless you are prepared. Go to meetings to close deals. Let your others do the discussions and deals. Just sign papers and thank the participants. Your ideas should be unifying, and not divisive. What matters is what your people wish. Do the will of those you serve—your people—if you want to be a good queen. Do not laugh out loud in public. Just wave and smile.

Every morning, obtain a summary of the world news from your staff. You may watch the Oprah show, but without commercials. Watch TV if you are in the program; if not, read a book.

Sponsor teachers to come to the USA, or award a trip to the USA. Introduce and fund after-school programs. Smart citizens are usually more productive. You do not want to be a queen over a dump nation. Read the Bible before you go to church on Sundays. You do not want the preacher to confuse or surprise you. Always be on time for the service. Stand up to thank God for making it possible for you to be there. Pray that you see more Sundays. This is a special day, where you thank the Lord for last week, and prepare yourself for the following week.

Support your brothers and sisters. However, don't interfere with their businesses. You may give them your recommendations. Take care of Thabiso (Beans). You have taken a lot from me and very little was left for him. He should marry someone in the medical field. He is going to need a registered nurse (RN) or a doctor for his short fuse.

I want a true princess for him. I want somebody that will fall in love with all of us, not just him. How can anyone say they love my son without loving his family? Anyone who wants any of you should want all for us. We do not get traded like ballplayers. I love my son, and will love his family.

Go shopping with Thabang. She has a hard time choosing clothes. Make sure she gets nothing but the best. Interview all her boyfriends. Nobody should take advantage of her good heart. I leave her the house next to yours. Never go to bed without giving her a hug or a call. She has to feel that you are there for her, like I was. Tell her I said she should do sports medicine and marry a ballplayer.

Provide a bodyguard for her and her husband. I would like the husband to be either a Catholic or Anglican. He is going to have to learn how to be a prince. He should never raise his voice. He should be involved in building communities. He should be a winner. His limo should fly a Bochabela flag. He should also listen to country music. It's good for the nerves.

Lehloa (Little Man) is trouble. You might have to call him every hour to make sure he has not taken off with a Spanish girl. However, I love him so much I named him after me. He is my mini me. I wanted him to be like me. Actually, when I look in his eyes I laugh because I see myself. Every day he is a reminder that I am alive.

I wish that I could take everything that is inside of me and give it to him. If I could, I would live with him forever. I love him very much. There is nothing that he does or that he will do that I cannot understand. Since he is a mini version of me, he will do everything just as I remember. If he does something wrong, I will be sad for him because I know he tries to do his best. I never want to see his tears, because this I cannot handle. If he cries after I spank him, I also go to my room and cry my eyeballs out.

I love him, feel for him and wish all good things for him. He walks in my footsteps. All his strange manners, it's me all over again. It's like watching your film; it keeps getting closer and closer. I cannot remember all the parts until he acts them out. He is the story of my life, life in living color, and I don't want it to end.

I have opened an account for him. I want you to use it to buy him a house as a wedding present. Then just maintain the account in case he needs some help. I am giving him our first auto dealership and the repair shop. I want him to concentrate on designing and building cars.

WHAT I WOULD LEAVE FOR MY FAMILY

Let the managers run the dealership. Remember that all of the money should be kept in the family bank. You will all share the profits equally. All major expenses should be paid from one account. I don't want Thabiso to pay his own utilities. Find a way to make it work. Little Man, just build cars; do not race them. You also must have a driver and a bodyguard. Hire Frank as your bodyguard. You are going to spend a lot of time together anyway.

I leave you the downtown house. This should make it harder for you and your friends to make noise. Also, I don't want you to bring work home. The house has seven bedrooms. Keep the staff. If you look after them, then they will take good care of you. I want you to welcome all of our important guests. Be the man. This is what I would do so good luck and represent. Senate will help you with the details.

Always wear a suit when you go to work. Do not handle any cash. Let the workers deal with it. Before you make a large purchase, run it by Senate. If she approves, then you are in good shape. That means do not hide things from each other.

Work to have fun. Once a week meet with the mayor or the governor. Know your politics well. Care about the health and well-being of the city. Do not run for office, and do not join a political party. You were born to be a king. That means you represent all the people, all of the time.

When the campaigns are over, the winners will ask you what is next or what they should do. Tell them to do the will of the people that they serve. The voters are always right. If you do not want to do their will, then let someone else represent them. The people will make you their king, if you serve them sincerely. Remember they come first. Your time is their time. You will have no vacation. Well, unless they all have jobs. Would you let your servant take a vacation before the work is done? Remember you work for them. They will let you know when to take a break. It will take more than your good looks to be a king. It will take hard work, commitment, character and a lot of praying. Good luck, my king.

In your kingdom, there will be no project housing. In your kingdom, there will be no homeless people. You will find jobs for them or create them. Do not be afraid to be a "champion of the people." Provide training and open factories. It will take time, but you should stay with the program, even if you are only able to take one family out of the projects at a time. Those you serve will call you their king.

After twelve years of school, the students should obtain a certificate of some kind. They could learn auto mechanics, carpentry, dog grooming, ROTC, or whatever can provide them a job. After high school, they should all be employable. If they want to continue with a college level degree, power to them! It will mean more money. Your sister is about to finish high school, but she cannot even drive a car to deliver pizza. Let us hope she does well in college or marries a rich prince. It's okay, because I love her. I will make sure that she is successful, because that is my job and I enjoy it.

Since you are going to need all the help you can get, I suggest we go to South Africa to find you a wife. You need somebody from the royal family. Someone raised to serve her people. She has to be tall. Her people should see her coming from far, or be able to pick her out in the crowd. We have to start looking now, because this is going to be a special princess. God has blessed me with your mother. I pray that you find somebody that loves you and your people. We might have to send her to college to study government. She is going to have to deal with the elected representatives. We are looking for a beautiful, tall and intelligent princess.

If you marry someone from here, then she might leave you at home, alone and go on vacation in Aruba. Your princess must share our vision. If not, then "Houston", you will have a problem. It is going to take more than love to keep her. She must be dedicated like Mrs. Martin Luther King, yet tough and smart like Senator Hillary Clinton. If it were up to me, I would make the senator a queen of a small country. Her desire to serve is as if she grew up in a royal family. Conditioned to do nothing but serve the people. Every time I see her, I wonder what she is planning. She has such a sharp and powerful mind. If you need knowledge, ask those who have it. So if you have a question about policy, give her a call. Tell her I sent you.

This country does not show much appreciation for their leaders. Where I come from, leaders of a country are its treasure. Here, you are either a Republican or Democrat. You can be a very good lawyer or judge, but because you are a Republican, there must be something wrong with you. So they will work day and night to defeat your nomination. Any leader should be given a chance to speak as long as they want with no labels and interruptions.

I would love to sit and listen to Justice Clarence Thomas. When is he going to speak at Howard University School of Law? He could go there at lunchtime. Speak for half an hour, have lunch and go back to work. Well, maybe somebody is afraid of what he will say or teach us. So they are keeping him away from us. Who is best suited to explain to our youth in high school or college the importance of knowing and following the law? I would like to hear him address his people even if it is one time only. I wonder if the NAACP ever invited him to speak. Those who have something of substance to say are "blocked" at every turn. Those who have nothing that we can use or learn from are given the loudest microphones.

Little Man, admire and learn from those who are above you. Respect and honor all leaders, especially those who are not given a chance to speak, or communicate freely. Remember, an empty bucket makes the loudest noise. Wisdom is not kept in one head or political party. Listen to everyone and do not belong to a political party. Always have a guest at your dinner table. Listen and you might learn something. Remember when you speak, you are only repeating what you know or hear.

Avoid TV shows. They only play with your mind while wasting your precious time. If bored, call somebody, or write a letter instead of being a puppet with a remote control. What can you learn from a show designed solely to amuse you? Go to classical concerts—you might meet some interesting people. There is no one to meet when watching TV. You may watch PBS. Give yourself an hour for the staff to bring you up to speed with the world news, national and local news. Let them research the news and give you a summary. Also, obtain an update of the family businesses.

I leave you the company jet. Make sure that it is well maintained and use it only for business. No fun trips to some unknown island and getting lost. You may have to fly Amohelang (Skudy-Skudy) to her golf tournaments. Whenever you can, go with her and support her.

Don't have more than three children, also. You will have a hard time finding time for all of them. Keep them close to you, and teach them about their grand father King Morara II. Wear comfortable shoes. You might have to stand and give an hour-long speech or walk for a mile. Always drive your wife to church every Sunday. You do not want the devil to find her at home watching R-rated movies. Love her like your best friend. Never put her in a tight spot or leave her hanging. Buy her shoes, even though she is sure to return them. Tell her you love her every day. Complement her especially when things did not go her way. Ask for her help regularly even if you can handle it by yourself. Make her part of your decision-making process. If you can sell it to her, you should have no problem with anyone else. Always value her opinion.

Never ask her what is for dinner, unless she's getting ready to bring it. Always tell her you are hungry, and finish your food; however, no seconds. Wash her feet at least once a week. This could lead to wonderful things. Ask her if you could comb her hair, of which she will say no! But she will be happy you asked. However you can, show her you have time for her. Select clothes for her to wear, even though you cannot match a t-shirt and jean outfit. That way, when she appears with something different, you can say, "Wow! You go, Mrs. So-and-so!" Then ask her to be your date and promise to be a good boy.

Always allow her to finish her sentence. Do not interrupt, especially when you think she is wrong. Be a good listener and participant. Write her parents and tell them that she is okay, and that she is the best thing that ever happened to you. Take responsibility when things get messy. Never raise your voice in her presence. Who wants to see an angry husband? Never tell her how hard you worked or how tired you are. She is your queen and knows how hard you work for her. Just keep doing a good job and you will be rewarded.

Always tell the truth even if it scares you. It is hard to be up-front because the answer might be no. Sometimes no is a good answer because it may mean you are requesting something you cannot afford or are not ready for. For example, if you ask for a loan from a bank, and they tell you no, say thank you and then go home and save the money. You should always pay your own way. Have no debts and do not make loans. Whatever is in your possession should be paid in full.

Pray before you go to bed. Thank God for the opportunities that He has given you. Thank Him for the life you have. Thank Him for who you are. Thank Him for everything that He has given you: those you see, and those you cannot remember. Thank Him for the weather, for the air, for water and for good food. Ask Him to bless you with wisdom.

Ask Him to bless your family especially your wife. Thank Him for blessing you with her, and ask Him to keep her with you for a while. Thank Him for giving her patience to deal with your antics. Thank Him for making her so beautiful and smart. Thank Him for her love for you, when you cannot find anything for anybody to love about you. Ask God to give you special love just for her. Ask Him to open your mind and eyes to enjoy her presence and beauty. Ask Him to teach you how to appreciate her. Thank Him for her company and promise to care and cherish her.

Always sleep at home. If you have to go on a trip, do not leave her. Wherever you go, she should be welcome. Keep her well-informed. One day she might have to represent you. Do not stay too long in the military. It is a lot of fun and you can make good friends. But I think you can serve your community better as a civilian. You can open factories and provide training. Do not work for a private company. Open your own company and provide jobs for others.

Have lunch with one of your sisters or brother at least once a week. Listen to them, so you will know where the problems are. Call Senate at least once a day. She is going to need your help. She might be having problems with her family. Give special attention to Thabang. She works better in a group setting. Be there so she knows things are going to be okay. Go to the games to support her husband. Sometimes he will lose a game, so be there for moral support. Go golfing with her husband like your uncles Shelby and Rod did. Stay close to him and teach him how to be a good prince.

Look out for Thabiso (Beans). Do not let him borrow your car, because he might keep it. He may take some of your clothes. Once a week take him out for dinner. Teach him everything you know about the business. Talk to him often so he does not drive his wife crazy. He is very demanding, so keep up with him. Make sure that his wife and your wife go shopping together regularly. Praise his wife and love her like your sister. She is now a Moshoeshoe. Keep your brother in line. Make sure that he treats her nicely. She will be okay once they have children. Protect her and love her. When she is happy, she will take care of your brother. Your brother is just more active than some of us. He is a tiny- mini me, and I love him very much.

When he was sick and hospitalized, I cried uncontrollably. He was not in pain, but I just kept crying. It makes me mad when you guys get sick. I cry because there is nothing that I can do in most cases. I love your brother. He is always trying to make me laugh. He always says, "Yes, Daddy," or "No, Daddy." Other people just say, "Huh!" And I have to remind them to say, "Daddy."

I think Beans should have the other dealership. What do you think? Maybe he should continue running the pharmacy store. Yes, I think that will keep him busy. Make sure he is present in all the meetings. I have an account you can use to hook him up. Give him money before he asks for it. He might ask for a million, and you only have half. I think that he should get the minivan. Do not give him anything faster. His wife should drive the latest 800 series BMW. Also, they should have my S600. It's too luxurious, so he won't speed.

WHAT I WOULD LEAVE FOR MY FAMILY

His wife should only work part-time at the hospital. Check on Beans regularly and take him shopping. Make sure that she has an assistant and a bodyguard. Invite his wife's family for a weekend or a week. Make sure that they are well taken care of. I am leaving them the country house. It is nice and quiet out there. That should slow your brother down. We need to work on improving his patience.

Beans, I do not want you to leave school until you are a doctor. You shall be called Prince Thabiso Cowson Moshoeshoe, MD. I do not know why you should be a doctor, but this is how I feel. Love your wife, like I love your mother. Do not worry if she wants to win all of the arguments. Tell her that you love her even in your sleep. Appreciate her. Respect and protect her. Love her more each day. Build her love like you are building a mansion. Be deliberate. Make it your mission to love her. Never take her for granted. Always let her take the last bite or have the last word, unless she says, "I love you." Then you have got to say, "I love you more than I did yesterday."

Be by her side, and be assuring. She's now a Moshoeshoe, and must feel proud. Do not say negative things about her friends. Be strong for her, like a captain faced with a storm. All on board believe he is the only one who can save them from the storm. This is the only job I want you to do, and that is, love your wife. She is your princess; treat her well, and she will call you her prince. Watch your brother (Little Man), and learn from him. Make sure that he does not take off with the company jet.

AMOHELANG (SKUDY-SKUDY)

To my Skudy-Skudy (Amohelang), I love you seven hundred times. You are the only girl who can give me the look which melts my heart. You are one beautiful young woman. You have my oriental eyes, but your mother's feet, with long toes like fingers. Like Senate, I have the shortest toes on the planet. Good thing I do not wear open-toed shoes.

Keep working hard on your golf. If any woman can do it, you can. If you do not want to practice medicine full-time, that is okay with me. Play golf and have fun. It is a sport for princes and princesses. No chasing the ball up and down the court. Just strike the ball and stroll leisurely down the fairway. Remember to wave to the fans, because they are there to see you. Hopefully, you will win a few tournaments. You may use the company jet. I will come as often as I can to watch you. I love you with all my heart. I wish you to grow strong and more beautiful. You are the only one who comes to keep me company. Even your mother avoids me nowadays.

I leave you my five-bedroom condo downtown, so you may keep an eye on your brother. He might think he is me. So when his head gets too big, remind him that he is not me. He's just named Wycliffe after me. I love him. He is my mini-me. Take good care of him. His wife will need your support. Show her around and teach her the American ways. Take her to the tournaments. She's a good girl, but she just might be experiencing a culture shock.

Take her shopping, but no tight jeans. You also might learn something from her. Be good friends with Thabiso's wife. She is going to need all the help she can get. Take her side even when you think she is wrong. When a friend makes a mistake, you do not think they have done a permanent job. You forgive them and make them feel better again.

I would like you to hold the family together. Therefore, I leave you the restaurant, the sport store and the dry cleaners. When you are on tour, have Thabiso's wife keep an eye on things. I think that you should marry a chef. Make sure that he does not drink or smoke. It is okay if you have more than three children. If you have a daughter, name her Mamosilo or Tsidii. Mathabo would be nice also. Name your son Tsetsebe.

Make sure you take a bodyguard on tour. I do not want anything to happen to my Skudy-Skudy. I have opened an account for you to use after you get married. Remember you need a man that can cook. After chasing the children and golf, you will be too tired to cook.

Gather the family regularly at the restaurant. Talk to your sisters at least once a day. Do not let them boss you around. You are all equal partners. Get along for the family's sake. Mark your mother's birth date on your calendar. This will be a holiday for the family. Call it Masenate's day. Invite all of the Masenates to the party.

Respect and love each other as I love you. You are who you are, because of your family. The best gift God gave me is my family. I do not see what my purpose would be without you. You have put meaning into my life. Whenever I think of you, my heart fills up with joy. A hug from you surpasses all the riches of this world. I am always eager to come home, because it is the only place where I can find genuine peace.

I am proud and grateful to be your daddy. You make each day feel like my birthday or Fathers' Day. You have honored me with your kindness, politeness, respect, good hearts, and unselfishness. You have made me the proudest father in the whole world. The love I have for you will never change, and there is nothing you can do that could change my mind. There is nothing you can do that I would not understand. I will help you even if it means losing my right arm. My arm is just that, an arm. However, you, on the other hand, are the meaning of my life.

I am sorry that I did not get you pets when you were young. I guess I was too selfish. I was afraid you would spend more time with your pets than me. You are all beautiful people. Thabang (Bang-

Bang), take care of your aunt Amy and grandmother. Senate take care of everyone in Africa. You are now Ms. Africa. You are the queen. Lehloa (Little Man), look after your uncles, Peter and Shelby. Take them to watch Skudy-Skudy's golf tournaments. Thabiso (Beans), take care of your uncle Phillip (Mike Henry) and your uncle Thabiso (in South Africa), because Bonang, Sentso and Tsidii might give him headache. Every year make sure you visit him or bring him to the United States for a vacation. My Princess Amohelang (Skudy-Skudy) take care of your aunts; Dee-Dee, Margaret, Coco, April and Bobbie. Take them shopping or to have their nails done and get a new hairdo. Once a week, send someone to go and do their groceries and to help with cleaning. When you help others, God will reward you.

Senate, this moment is very hard for me to phrase because I do not know the day or hour that I am leaving. So allow me to put it this way, "Before I go, I would like to give you all my blessings—Then, Thabang, Lehloa, Amohelang, Thabiso and Laura—in that order." Take care of my babies, and love them even when they think they are better than you.

TO MY BROTHERS AND SISTERS

To Prince John Masia Moshoeshoe

You are like a father to me.
You made me feel safe.
You were always calm.
You never shouted at anyone in my presence.
You were always building a consensus.

You make everyone feel important.
You befriended and talked to everyone.
You sung in a choir and kept us entertained.

You always put yourself last.
You helped your friends.
You laughed and smiled away from trouble.

I am the shouting kind, but my son Lehloa is soft-spoken and calm
like you.
Everyday my house is full with his friends.
He is always bringing somebody from school.
I am glad that I know who he resembles; otherwise, I would go nuts.
Like you, nothing seems to bother him.

You are very kind.
I remember you used to send me money when I was in high school,
without questions.
It seems like everything you do, you do it for everyone but yourself.
You are a good servant to your people.
You are the best prince.

I hope that it won't be long before we get together and just chill or hang out.

I do not know what will happen after death, but I know for sure that I will be looking for you.

I hope that they have loving and helpful angels like you. If not, heaven will be a lonely place.

If I go before you, please call the heavens and tell them to open up for your little brother.

When I get there, I will rent an apartment where we can stay together.

If you go first, I will continue your good works, while looking forward to meeting you.

Thank you again for being there for me.

Thank you for being proud of me.

Thank you for being my big brother.

I love you, man!

WHAT I WOULD LEAVE FOR MY FAMILY

TO PRINCE SAMUEL HLALEFO MOSHOESHOE

May you always be honest.
May you always seek the truth.
May you always fight injustice.
May you always be uncompromising when it comes to justice.

It's a pity that I never had a chance to teach you how to cheat or lie.
If you want to know how honest my brother is, listen to this:
He is so honest that he would write himself a speeding ticket.
I can see him driving up to a state trooper and saying,
"I am sorry I have been speeding."

May you always be caring for your family and others.
May you always be a champion of the little or defenseless people.
May you always love God.
May you always enjoy a loud and uninhibited laughter.

You have always tolerated me, and I appreciate that.
Thank for giving me your favorite silk underwear.

I am sorry I missed your wedding.
When I get to heaven, I hope they allow wedding parties, because
I plan on throwing you the biggest party that heaven has ever seen.

Nurture and guide my children when I am gone.
I hope that your wife and children appreciate what you do for them.
I hope to keep your honesty and integrity until we meet.

Although it's our custom, I never called you "Abuti."
So, Abuti Sam, I love you, man!

TO PRINCE RORISANG OTLAIPONELA
MOSHOESHOE

I am sorry I missed your wedding.
I love your wife 'Mamosa, and your beautiful daughter Mosa, with her Asian eyes.
I love you, man!

I hope that you give me a chance to take care of you.
When we meet, I will not let you out of my sight.
I don't know how heaven will handle it, because it looks like they call us one at a time.
Well, I do not plan on leaving you again.

Do not despair, because help is on the way.
You are my handsome prince.

Do you remember how I used to walk you to school?
Do you remember when we walked down the hill, past some apartments, across a highway, and into a police camp, where your kindergarten school was located?
It was far, but we had fun along the way.

I remember when you used to let only me comb your hair.
I remember when you were as cute as a button.
In my heart I sincerely believe that I will get another chance to be with you.
We can walk your daughter to school together.
I love you, man!

WHAT I WOULD LEAVE FOR MY FAMILY

TO PRINCESS PORTIA LISEBO MOSHOESHOE

You should have been the boy that my father wanted, and
I should have been the girl that my mother wanted.

After my two older brothers John and Samuel, my mother and my
grandmother prayed for a girl. But nobody cared to inform my father,
who had made a deal with God that he wanted only boys.

You can imagine how sad or surprised my mother and grandmother
were when I was born, because they were sure that I was going to be
a baby girl. My father was very happy, but surprised that my mother
was not so happy. So he asked them, "Why is everyone so gloomy?"
They told him that they have been praying for a girl. Then he told
them, "Well, God answered my prayer because I asked him to give me
only boys."

After a family meeting, my father agreed with them, and they all
prayed for a girl. Thus, I was named Liteboho, which would be a
prayer every day they call my name, to remind God that they have
enough boys and are praying for a girl. So, my baby sister, that's why
you were born after me.

You were given the name Lisebo, which means "whispering" or "gossiping," because the village was gossiping or talking about how our
family was praying and expecting a girl. Out of fear of witchcraft, you
were taken away from the village.

You grew up somewhere that I didn't know.
You never went to the same primary schools that I attended.
You never played the games that the village girls played.

You never learned how to balance a bucket of water on your head like the women in the village.

I never had to protect my only baby sister from a school bully.
I never had a chance to carry your books from school.
I never had a chance to buy you snack at school during lunchtime.
I never had a chance to tell somebody off and say, "That's my sister, and if you touch her, I will break your...you know what!"
I never had a chance to carry you on my back on the way from school.
I never had a chance to show you how much I love you.

You never had a chance to cry for my toys and get me in trouble.
You never got a chance to tell on me.
I never had a chance to run away with your dolls while you chase me yelling, "Mom, Mom! Give it back! Give it back!"

By the time I got close to you, you were in high school, and I was in college.
Now when I try to play big brother, all you get from me is a lecture, "Do this, do that, or no! Why? Or stop, stop!"
There is no "I love you. Give me a hug."

I hate witches and their witchcraft, because if it weren't for them running you off,
I would have had a baby sister.
I would be enjoying our young, but old memories.
We would have been a team, just like me and my older brothers.

How can I rebuild our relationship?
What am I going to build it on?
I am confused and frustrated.

If you find yourself running with the wrong group and getting in trouble, it is not your fault, my dear sister. It only points out that I am not there.

WHAT I WOULD LEAVE FOR MY FAMILY

I am not there to walk you to your college dorm.
I am not there to drive you to your first job interview.
I am not there to bottle your boyfriend and tell him, "If you touch my sister, I will…"

When you get fired from work for being late, it is not your fault, my baby sister.
It only means that I was not there to drive you or teach you how to drive.
I was not there to take you to lunch and make you late for work.
I was not there to hug you when life was giving you headache.
I was not there to wipe you tears when you felt bad.

When you were expecting, I never saw your big stomach.
I never drove you to the doctor's office for checkup.
I never met your son until he had already finished high school.

May the Lord give me an opportunity to spoil you with presents and stuff!
I would like to take you to get your hair and your nails done.
I can't wait to take you abroad.
It's your choice, but I think we should start in Australia, Europe, Canada, New York, DC, Florida, California, then Ethiopia, Egypt, Botswana, Bloemfontein, and finally Maseru.

I think we will be old and broke by the time we finish. However, we will be happy!
I love you, baby sister.

Pack your suitcase, because Sydney, here we come!

TO THE PASTOR WHO PRAYED FOR MY SON WHEN HE WAS SICK

Dear Pastor,

I would like to thank you for praying for my son Thabiso Cowson Moshoeshoe. He was very sick. He had some bumps and swelling on his face. I took him to St. Mary's Hospital in Richmond, Virginia. The doctors ran every possible test they could, but no one could tell us what caused the illness. He was placed in an isolation ward for about two days. Still his face grew bigger and bigger. I could hardly see his eyes. The doctors had no answer and could not give him drugs because the lab tests revealed nothing.

I work in Northern Virginia, so I had to call my boss to tell him that I could not come to work because my son was very ill. Even though my son told me that he was not in pain and tried to smile for me, I just kept on crying whenever I turned away from him. I was desperate and angry. I did all that I could, which was to rush him to the hospital. Nothing made sense to me. I was mentally paralyzed. The only thing I could do, or that happened was I could not stop crying. I tried to block it out of my mind, but my son was there, in front of me, with a round face, and could hardly see. My wife stayed overnight. That gave me a break.

There were many things I have asked my boss. I have worked with him for three years, but he is yet to promote me to a management position. Anyway, after I called him and told him about my son's problem, he promised me that he would call his pastor to pray for my son. I told him "Thank you sir," and felt like he gave me the promotion that I had been asking for.

When I called him, it was early in the morning. I do not know when he called you, but when I came back from lunch with my daughter Senate, my son had been transferred to another room he shared with another little boy. I asked my wife, "Masenate, what happened?" and she said, "He just started getting better." He had improved so much that the doctor said that he could be released. Indeed, later that evening he was sent home.

I have never been so happy in my life. I kept telling the doctors and the RNs, "Thank you, thank you." After we got home, little Thabiso had a smooth cute little face I know. Then I remembered the promise my boss made, that he would call you, to pray for my son. The prayer worked! The prayer succeeded where doctors could not.

It took me a few days to understand what had happened. I was in trouble, frustrated, lost, and desperate, but a man I do not know, never saw, and does not know me, asked his God to heal my son. The only thing I was sure about was that my boss would not let me down. He will call his pastor. I had no doubt about it. He may forget to promote me, but this one thing, he will do for me. I am glad I came to America. I am glad I have a boss who cares. I am glad he is a Christian.

This situation, act, or miracle with my son showed me God's kindness. It showed me His mercy. It showed me his power. It showed me his unconditional love. God did for me what doctors could not do. He loves my family, but I had no idea about His mercy and power. However, on that day I saw His work.

I thank God for giving me a son that I love very much. When he was very ill, your prayers healed him. You spoke to your God about a little boy from a small country somewhere in Africa, and He heard your prayers, and my son was healed. This is the best lesson that I have found in America.

I pray that I never forget what God did for me and my boy, so that one day, I may return to my village, point to my son, and say, "I was in America, and I saw God's power." My son is the evidence that God is compassionate, that He is able, and that He hears one's prayers. Every time I hug my son, I am reminded of God's love. Through my son's healing, my eyes and my heart have been opened to love and to have trust in Him.

Pastor thank you for caring. Thank you for being my boss's friend, and thank you for your prayers.

TO MY FATHER(S)

Mr. Thabiso W. Moshoeshoe

- He believes in God 100 percent.
- He has 200 percent faith in God.
- He is truthful and sincere 100 percent.
- He is 300 percent times happy.
- He loves me 600 percent.
- I am 105 percent sure that he loves and obeys God.
- I love him very much.
- Sorry Dad I joined the Navy instead of the Army. Go Navy!

Mr. Cowson Seipobi

- He loves me 110 percent.
- He taught me everything I could learn about business.
- He taught me to be strong.
- I will go with him, anywhere, anytime and face anybody or anything.
- There is not anything that he could do or say that I would not understand.
- I support him 100 percent.
- I will not engage in any business operations without his advice.
- He taught me everything I am ever going to need to be strong.
- I love him 700 percent.
- Dad I hope you don't mind if I keep your white shirt.

Mr. Tlelai

- He taught me respect.
- He taught me clearness.
- He taught me confidence.
- He taught me generosity.
- He taught me to love.
- He loves me and he loves me
- He gave me an education.
- He paid or bought me things that no one would have offered me.
- He raised me like building a house from the ground up.
- He taught me to understand money and its importance in life.
- He taught me to be calm when things do not go my way.
- He taught me to be a good citizen.
- He taught me to think methodically.
- He taught me to put God first in everything I do.
- He taught me to be nice to everyone.
- Therefore I love him with all my heart.
- Sorry Dad I still do not know how to drive a manual or stick shift.

TO MY MOTHER(S)

(Mapotlaki, Mamoroka, and Matumo)

Thank you, and thank you for having me.
Thank you for being there to hold me when it was cold.
Thank you for proudly carrying me everywhere that you went.
To you I was always a shining star.

You held me when I was crying.
You held me when I had a fever.
Not even my stinks deterred you.
You just smiled and congratulated me for a job well done.
Then you cleaned me and left me smelling like roses.

Thank you for patiently carrying me around for nine long months.
Your enemies thought your were carrying a monster, but you thought
of me as an angel.
I know you are still waiting for me to become one.

Thank you for wanting me even after you already had my two older
brothers.
Thank you for continuing to feed me even when I kept spitting or
just playing.
Thank you for being there; to hold me, to sing for me, to teach me
how to talk and how to walk.

You proudly held my hand and encouraged me to take my first step.
I do not know how many times I fell, but you never gave up on me.
Since I can remember, you have never stopped caring or looking after
me.

I am like a house that one never finishes building, cleaning, maintaining,
worrying about, or paying for.

I wonder if you will ever sit down to enjoy me, if you will ever stop worrying about me.
I have no idea what makes you happy or what I can do to show you my appreciation.
All of my life I have been running away from you. From when I was growling, and when I started walking. I used to hide from you. Now I am old, and what do you know? I left the country! Maybe all you ever wanted was to sit down and enjoy my presence.
Maybe you just wanted to spend a little time talking to me.
As you were molding me, I grew bigger, heavier, taller, stronger, and naughtier I must add.

I wonder how much of your teaching is within me.
I know you pointed me in the right direction, because I made it through the first grade, high school, college and boot camp.

I wonder how it felt like when you took me for my first day to school.
What did it feel like when you had to leave me at school?
How worried were you?
Did you go home and relax for the first time after so many months of coaching, cleaning and baby talking? Or did you stare at the clock and wish it could move faster? Or perhaps it looked like it would stop?
Did you shake it and put it to your ear to find out if it was running?

You have given me so much love.
How can I ever repay you?
How can I give you the same love?
Is it possible to trade places?

WHAT I WOULD LEAVE FOR MY FAMILY

Can I walk you to school, then return home only to worry about you?

Can I stay up all night long when you are sick?

Can I at least wash your feet and comb your hair, and maybe do your nails?

Can I cook lunch for you and watch you take a small bite and say you lost your appetite?

Would I still love you if you broke my favorite dishes or wrote on my walls?

What about if you took my sports car without my permission, and ran it into a pole?

Would I still love you if you paid me no mind and mumbled something as you walk out?

How would I feel if you came home late and had not called? Or did not come home at all?

Would I stay and wait for you all night long and pray that you come back safe?

I guess becoming you would be a miracle.

Mapotlaki, thank you for sowing my first Boy Scout uniform.

Mamoroka, thank you for buying me a red sweater or jersey.

Matumo, thank you for sending me cash in an envelope when I was in college, and thank you also for driving me to St. Monica's Leribe.

You all have done more for me than I can ever repay or recount.

I love you dearly. Among all your children, you have always made me feel special.

I am very proud to be your number one son, and I am unanimous when I say,

"I love you more than your other children." I am glad to have three wonderful moms.

I thank God for blessing me with you.

I thank Him for making it possible for you to take care of me.

I am glad God gave me a chance to say, "Mom, thank you for everything.

You are truly the best, and I love you very much."

TO MASENATE

Give me your hand because you are coming with me. I do not know if heaven knows how I like my pancakes. I am sorry I love you so much that I cannot leave you. If you are not ready, I will tell the angels to come back later, after you finish watching *Judge Mathis Show* or your favorite police show. I am the luckiest man to be your husband. If you would like to know how I love her:

I Love Her the Way She Is

When I hold you in my arms over and over, I forget about the dirty dishes in the sink. I forget about the pile of dirty laundry. I forget about the living room. When you lay beside me, everything is perfect. My world becomes perfect. I forget about car payments, loans, mortgages, and school fees. The more we dance hand in hand, the more I love you.

When I am with you, I cannot hear the kids play. Why did you have to be alone in the delivery room? I was afraid you would see me crying. I was afraid I could not control my love for you. I hope that you never jump over the cliff, because I will follow you.

These are the things that I would like to know. Are you okay? Would you like to sit down? May I take off your shoes? May I get you something to drink? How was your day? Would you like to take a nap?

You look nice, but you should go shopping tomorrow. If there is something that you would like, then I hope you tell me. You do a good job. You have beautiful children. I hope that they grow up to be like you, especially our two boys.

I have no question in my mind that you love me. I hope that you know that you are number one in my life, and that I love you. I love you when dinner is not ready. I love you when you forget to buy toilet paper. I love you when you are running late for school or church. I love you when you play your music loud. I love you when you don't make sense.

I love you when you come late from your mother's house. I love you when you wear something that I don't like. I love you when you snore. I love you when you give me leftovers. It's okay if you kiss me with garlic breath. I will still kiss you after you eat pig's feet. I love you when you get mad at me for no reason. For twenty years I have loved you. So please don't change.

The look in your eyes makes me feel safe. It makes me feel warm, calm and joyful. It's like the feeling you get when a baby is looking at you. I cannot think of you doing anything to harm me.

When I talk loud and tell long stories, I do that to draw your love. When you hear me calling, "Masenate! Masenate!" It is because I am already missing you. If there is such a thing as forever, I will love you forever and ever.

Many wonderful things you have done for me and our family, I have forgotten, but I still would like to thank you. Thank you for loving me. Thank you for our three girls and two boys. Thank you for taking them to school. Thank you for taking them to the doctor. Thank you for taking them to church. Thank you for laughing and playing with them. Thank you for taking them to the park. Thank you for taking them to the pool. Thank you for being there when they need you. Thank you for thinking that I am beautiful, and mistaking me for a girl when we first met. Thank you for being my friend. I hope that you will remain beside me forever.

I am glad that you chose me. I am glad that you married me. I am glad that you kept me. Most of all, I am glad that you are my babies' mama. If you know, please tell me how to thank you. If you know, please tell me how to love you.

In my eyes, you will always be young, beautiful and sexy. You will always be in my heart. When you are sad, I am sadder. When you are happy, I am dancing. You are sexy every hour on the hour. Good or bad, you are my only habit. To the world, you are the most beautiful of women. I wish that your shoes are always soft and comfortable. I wish that you do not have to work. I wish that you could take long naps and talk on the phone for hours when you wake up. I wish that your hair were always perfect. I wish that you could travel in your own jet. I wish that everyone was nice to you. I wish that I could be there anytime that you needed me.

There may be things that you did wrong or you wish you could change. I cannot remember them and I have not seen them. I don't remember even one sad moment with you. Not even one. When I seem angry, it's because I need a hug and a kiss. When I have received too much work from my boss lady, I look in your eyes, and I get energy to finish my work. When my eyes look at another lady, I quietly put your face on her and receive a clearer conversation.

I appreciate everything that you do for us. How can I please you? How can I make your days fun? How can I make your job easier? How can I make you feel content?

To our children: Senate (Tsompi-Tsompi), Thabang (Bang-Bang), Lehloa (Baby Brother), Amohelang (Skudy-Skudy), and Cowson (Beans). I love your mother, so please stop knocking at the door when it's closed.